airplane
sky.

is a balloon
I like to buy.

is a candle on a
birthday cake.

is a duck
swimming on
a lake.

is an eagle
perched high
in a tree.

Ff

is my family.
Mommy, Daddy
and me!

is a goose
that's waddling
along.

G g

is a horn singing a song.

Ii

is an ice
boat.

is s

jam

K k

is a a kangaroo
talking to a lamb!

is a lighthouse.

is a mouse.

is a robin's nest in the eaves of our house.

is an orange I
eat every day.

is a parrot that
says, "Fine, OK!"

is a pretty quilt.

Rr

is a rainbow
bright.

S s is a
tha

frisky squirrel
runs out of sight.

Tt

is a train
that runs on
a track.

is an umbrella standing in a rack.

Mother

is a valentine
I sent to my
mother.

W w

is a window
where I watch
for my brother.

is an
xylophone.

is a
yacht.